PRAYERS

of

Love

Contributing Writers

Nancy Parker Brummett

Lain Ehmann

Marie D. Jones

Publications International, Ltd.

Cover Photo: Shutterstock

Contributing Writers

Nancy Parker Brummett is a freelance writer, columnist, and the author of four books who lives in Colorado Springs, CO. Leading women closer to the heart of God is the hallmark of her speaking and writing ministries. To learn more about her life and work, visit www.nancyparkerbrummett.com.

Lain Ehmann is a Massachusetts-based writer and mom to three.

Marie D. Jones is the author of several best-selling nonfiction books and a contributing author to numerous inspirational books, including *Echoes of Love: Sisters, Mother, Grandmother, Friends, Graduation, Wedding; Mother's Daily Prayer Book;* and *When You Lose Someone You Love: God Will Comfort You.* She can be reached at www.mariedjones.com.

Acknowledgments

Louis Weber, CEO
Publications International, Ltd.
7373 North Cicero Avenue
Lincolnwood, Illinois 60712

GOD'S LOVE

God did not make us to walk through life alone, but to do so with the ones we love and care about. To love others, and have the experience of their love in return, is the highest expression of God's own love through us, his children. We reach out to others in friendship and find that we are never as alone as we thought.

Love may sometimes seem elusive, but God reminds us that once we open our own hearts to love, we find it waiting for us in those who come into our lives, ready to give of themselves. We find the right spouse to be our partner in life and the perfect friends to help us reach our goals and cheer us on when we feel like we can't continue.

God brings into our lives the people we need to make us be the best we can be and to open our hearts when we feel afraid to trust.

Love of others is a reflection of love of self, and in the eyes of those we love we see ourselves as we want to be: perfect, happy, filled with the joy of knowing that we are surrounded by the blessings of others who love us just as much as we love them. Through our relationships, we strive to become more and help those we care about become more as well. We give love and we receive it in return, and that is the way God intended us to live.

God, I thank you for the blessing of love from good friends. My friends shower me with love and care every day, and I feel comfort knowing they are always there for me. I am so grateful for each one of them, as different and unique as they are, and for the things they teach me. My friends are like gemstones, so priceless and beautiful. Thank you for friends old and friends new and for friends yet to come.

The second is this, "You shall love your neighbor as yourself." There is no other commandment greater than these.
—Mark 12:31

Lord, it has been said that it is better to give than to receive, and in no case is this more true than in the ability to love others. My heart fills with joy when I can offer support, share my skills or knowledge, or simply just be with someone in pain. This ability to love others is a gift from you and is but a taste of what awaits us in heaven. Thank you for giving us a glimpse of your kingdom, and thank you for allowing me to become part of your good works on earth. Amen.

God is love, and those who abide in love abide in God, and God abides in them. Love has been perfected among us in this: that we may have boldness on the day of judgment, because as he is, so are we in this world. There is no fear in love, but perfect love casts out fear; for fear has to do with punishment, and whoever fears has not reached perfection in love. We love because he first loved us.
—1 John 4:16–19

God, today I pray not for myself but for my friends and my family. I ask that you shine your loving light upon them for all the good they do. Bless them with all good things. Without my friends and family, I don't know how I would get by. I know in my heart that you sent each and every one of them to me; they were hand-picked by you with love. Bless my friends today. Amen.

*But you, O Lord, are a God merciful
and gracious, slow to anger and abounding
in steadfast love and faithfulness.
Turn to me and be gracious to me;
give your strength to your servant.*
—Psalm 86:15–16

Lord, there are times when it's easy for me to love the people I share my life with and times

when it's just so hard. On the difficult days,
Lord, I pray that you would help me love as
you love. I come to you to draw on your unending source of pure love, so that I can let my first
response to any situation be a response based
not on my own self-interest, but based on love.
Thank you, Lord, for loving us. If you didn't,
we'd never be able to love others in a way that
brings you glory.

 ⤛ ⤜

*Two are better than one, because they have a good
reward for their toil. For if they fall, one will lift
up the other; but woe to one who is alone and falls
and does not have another to help.*
—Ecclesiastes 4:9

 ⤛ ⤜

Dear Heavenly Father, you have commanded us
to act in love at all times. I want to obey you,
but I'm struggling. I am empty and tired, short

of patience and forgiveness. I need an extra
dose of your strength to help me. All good
things come from and through you, and I know
with your help I can go beyond myself and
reach a new reservoir of love within me. Please
be with me today as I face the challenges in my
life, reminding me that with you all things are
possible. Amen.

Sovereign Lord, as part of my spiritual journey
here on earth, I want to grow in my ability to
love and care for others. You have provided us
such a wonderful example in your Son, Jesus
Christ, and I ask that you help me follow in
his path, giving with all my heart to everyone
I encounter. Please continue to show me how
to develop my ability to love others, knowing what to offer them and how to meet their
needs. I ask in your name, Amen.

*If there is among you anyone in need, a member
of your community in any of your towns
within the land that the Lord your God
is giving you, do not be hard-hearted or
tight-fisted toward your needy neighbor.*
—Deuteronomy 15:7

Lord, today I ask you to be with all the parents-to-be who secretly worry, "What if I don't love this baby when it's born?" What a surprise they have in store, Lord! For from your bounty of love overflowing you always deliver a generous portion to each one. And when the second baby comes? You simply double the capacity for love. Thank you, Lord, for a parent's love. Something that pure and precious could only come from you. Amen.

Lord, love seems so hard sometimes. The ones I love often hurt me, and I am sure I am not always kind to them either. Help me understand them better and be kinder and more compassionate when they push my buttons and try my patience. I want to be a loving person, but I don't always feel so loving. I pray for the strength and patience to always choose love over anger, peace over turmoil. Thank you, dear God.

I know, O Lord, that your judgments are right, and that in faithfulness you have humbled me. Let your steadfast love become my comfort according to your promise to your servant.
—Psalm 119:75–76

I can tell you love me, Lord! I feel your presence today as I work. I see your answer to last week's prayer right before my eyes. I feel my spirit lifted when I sing praises to you as I drive in the car. You are behind me, before me, and in me. Wherever I go, I am surrounded by your love—love that knows no bounds and has no end. Thank you, Lord. All I can say is, "I love you, too!"

I pray that you may have the power to comprehend, with all the saints, what is the breadth and length and height and depth, and to know the love of Christ that surpasses knowledge, so that you may be filled with all the fullness of God.
—Ephesians 3:18–19

Holy God, you are so merciful and caring! You have filled me so entirely with your love that I cannot help but share it with others. I go through my days, amazed that you have

chosen me to help spread your Word. I delight
in helping others learn of your power and truth.
I am blessed by your existence, and I long only
to praise your name, letting others see the glory
of the miracles you have worked in me. Amen.

I give you a new commandment,
that you love one another.
Just as I have loved you,
you also should love one another.
—John 13:34

Dear Lord, my heart is feeling empty today,
and I long for a true love to come into my life.
Help me become the kind of person I look for
in another, a partner and companion that will
walk with me through life. Send me a love I
can trust and believe in, who will stand up for
me when the world threatens to push me down.

I believe that you have created someone special just for me, so please prepare me to receive that special person, that we may be together soon. Amen.

~ ~

Lord Jesus, how blessed we are that you left your heavenly kingdom to dwell among us and show us what real love looks like. Without your example, we'd still be looking for love in all the wrong places. Thank you, Lord, for keeping your instruction so simple to understand, even though it's often so hard to follow. Simply love one another, is that it? Okay, Lord, if you say so. It's the least we can do after all you've done for us.

~ ~

Dear Lord, I feel like I've been waiting forever for a true friend to share my life with. There are so many times when I feel alone in this big world. I want a companion to walk with, laugh with, and share hopes, fears, and disappointments with. Please help me find someone I can trust and love. And until I find that person, please remind me that I am never really alone because I have you, unconditionally and eternally. Amen.

Father, every time I think of your sacrifice for your human creations, I am overwhelmed. That you would give so much for us is almost inconceivable. There are no possible words to express the depth of love you have for us and no possible way to repay it. So I will simply say, "Thank you." Thank you for being our Father in heaven, and thank you for giving us the opportunity to love you in return. Amen.

God, they say you get by with a little help from your friends, and I know that to be true. Thank you for filling my life and my days with good friends who care about me. Each one is like an angel sent down from heaven in human form, and I cherish them all. So today I ask that you keep my friendships strong and true, no matter how much time or distance may separate us as we all live our lives. Keep them close where it counts—in my heart. Thank you.

No one has greater love than this,
to lay down one's life for one's friends.
—John 15:13

My life is filled with love today, and I have you to thank, God, for bringing into my world great family and friends. I could not have picked better myself. I am surrounded by love and care and never feel alone in the presence of those you have permitted to walk alongside me on the path of life. And on those few occasions when I am alone, I know that your love, God, is ever present and infinite, and I am at peace in my heart. Amen.

You shall love the Lord your God with all your heart, and with all your soul, and with all your mind, and with all your strength.
—Mark 12:30

and care never feel alone

Lord, I truly want to love you with all my heart, soul, mind, and strength—so why do I have such a hard time doing it? At times my heart is fully engaged in loving you, but my mind is struggling with unanswered questions. Some days my soul seems too weary to love, Lord, and my strength? Well, it's just not there.

Forgive me, Lord. It is my dearest desire to love you as totally as you deserve to be loved. Help me even in this, Lord.

God, they say all you need is love, and that is true. Your loving care has gotten me through so many lumps and bumps, and you continue to be there for me at each and every turn on the road of life. My heart shines with the love that never ceases, the love of you, my God, who always watches over me and makes clear my way. You take away my burdens and lighten my load, and your love smooths the path you have set out for me. Thank you, God.

Lord, what an amazing thing it is that pure love keeps no record of wrongs and is not resentful. Can you teach us to love like that, Lord? Instead, we so often go over and over

all the grievances we have toward our spouse,
child, or friend we love. Is it really possible to
tear up those records and look at the people
we love the way you look at us—as if we'd
never sinned? I believe it is, Lord, but only by
your power. Give us the strength to forget the
wrongs, let go of the resentments, and embrace
the love.

Love is patient; love is kind. . . .
It does not insist on its own way;
it is not irritable or resentful.
—1 Corinthians 13:4–5

Lord, the best way for me to love you is
through loving your creations. You have made
every good thing in this world, and it is our job
to love and care for all of them, great and small.
Please remind me today that the way I treat the

least of your creations is the way I worship you. Let me care for the people, animals, and things around me with a full heart, knowing that my actions reflect my love and appreciation for you. Amen.

★ ★

Lord, who can I give love to today? You have chosen to give me your love, and I want to share it with someone who could really use a little extra love. Please send them my way, and help me recognize them when I see them, so that I can be as much an angel to them as you have been to me. I feel as if I have enough love for the whole world to bask in, so help me spread love wherever I go today, especially to those who have given up hope and need it most of all. Amen.

★ ★

Lord, could you please help me love the unlovable? I know it isn't possible for me to do this alone, so allow me to see them through your eyes—as precious people created in your image. I know that in some ways we all look the same to you, Lord, even as you are so keenly aware of our differences. To you, we are all lovable. Give me eyes to see others that way too, Lord. Without you, it's simply not possible.

For God all things are possible.
—Mark 10:27

Jesus, when I wonder how best to teach others about you, the same answer comes to me. All I have to do is love them. Love is your first and best gift to us. To show others your true nature, I only have to love them the way you would—selflessly and generously. Just as Mary poured her precious oil over your feet, I need to pour my love over those in my life. Then they will be able to experience firsthand the generosity of Christ. Thank you for loving me, and in doing so, teaching me how to love others. Amen.

I came to you late, O Beauty so ancient and new. I came to love you late. You were within me and I was outside where I rushed about wildly searching for you like some monster loose in your beautiful world. You were with me but I was not with you. You called me, you shouted to me, you wrapped me in your Splendour, you broke past my deafness, you bathed me in your Light, you sent my blindness reeling. You gave out such a delightful fragrance and I drew it in and came breathing hard after you. I tasted, and it made me hunger and thirst; you touched me, and I burned to know your Peace.
—St. Augustine of Hippo

Almighty God, only you could be creative
enough to instill different passions in each of
us. We love music, teaching, traveling, writing,
singing—any number of pursuits—because you
created us to be drawn to them. How empty
life would seem without our passions! Don't let
me neglect the passions you've given me, Lord,
and most importantly, show me ways to pursue
them to your glory! Thank you, Lord, for filling
our hearts with passion for the things we love.

Give thanks to the Lord of hosts,
for the Lord is good,
for his steadfast love endures forever.
—Jeremiah 33:11

God, of all your precious gifts, love is the rar-
est and most precious of all. Too often I find
myself acting in ways that are unloving and

unkind. That is when I most need your love to remind me to stop and take a deep breath. Anger and hatred never solve any problems. Only love seems to make the rough spots smoother and the hard roads easier to walk upon. I ask that you continue to remind me of the power of love each day, especially when it seems so much easier to choose to be unkind.

Beloved, let us love one another,
because love is from God; everyone
who loves is born of God and knows God.
—1 John 4:7

Dear Lord, I think I'm doing a pretty good job on your commandment to love my neighbors. But loving my enemies—I'm stuck. I'm having so much trouble loving those I disagree with or dislike, or those who hurt me or who have done me wrong. Please help me see my way to dealing with them with compassion and love, despite my earthly emotions. If I can see them and their actions through your eyes, I will be able to treat them as cherished children of God who are, themselves, hurting and in need of love. That is such a tough order, and I can only do it with your help. Amen.

—— ✧ ——

Keep alert, stand firm in your faith,
be courageous, be strong.
Let all that you do be done in love.
—1 Corinthians 16:13

—— ✧ ——

The love you give me, God, can carry me through my life. I have no need for anything else, for with your love comes the kingdom and all that it offers. Your love is like the most priceless riches, a treasure trove that never ends

and always provides me with everything I need
to be happy, healthy, and free. I depend on your
love, and I share that love with those I come
in contact with, knowing that as I give, I shall
receive more. Your love is my treasure, God.
Thank you. Amen.

I'm hurt and angry today, Lord. Someone I
love has trampled on my heart and sinned
against me, and I'm not sure what to do about
it. I know I should love them anyway, but that
doesn't really come easily. Thank you, Lord, for
teaching us that it is possible to love the sinner
even when we hate the sin. You love me in spite
of all my sins and imperfections, so with your
help I will try to do the same. In my heart I
know there's no better response than love. May
it flow freely from me today, Lord. Amen.

*You have heard that it was said, "You shall love
your neighbor and hate your enemy." But I say to
you, Love your enemies and pray for those who
persecute you, so that you may be children of your
Father in heaven; for he makes his sun rise on
the evil and on the good, and sends rain on the
righteous and on the unrighteous. For if you love
those who love you, what reward do you have?
Do not even the tax collectors do the same? And if
you greet only your brothers and sisters, what more
are you doing than others? Do not even
the Gentiles do the same? Be perfect, therefore,
as your heavenly Father is perfect.*
—Matthew 5:43–48

Heavenly Father, when you came to earth to
show us how to live, you did so not for your
own glory, but out of love for us. In turn, your
rules are ways that you show your love, not an
attempt to control or thwart our free will. By
giving us guidelines, you are helping us live

fulfilling, spiritual, and safe lives. When I follow your commandments, it is a way of show-
ing you how much I love you in return. Please
help me remember how to love you every day.
Amen.

⤙ ⤚

Dear Lord, falling in love can be the most fan-
tastic feeling in the world, as we get wrapped
up in our beloved. But earthly infatuations fade,
and the real commitment comes from loving
day in and day out, through sickness and
health. When I fight my selfish impulses in
order to act loving toward the one I've made
a commitment to, I realize how much more
fulfilling *being* in love is than *falling* in love.
Thank you for allowing us to develop relationships and to learn how to love one another as
you love us—deeply and without reservation.
Amen.

⤙ ⤚

Love divine, all loves excelling,
joy of heav'n to earth come down,
Fix in us thy humble dwelling,
all thy faithful mercies crown.
Jesus, thou art all compassion,
pure, unbounded love thou art;
Visit us with thy salvation,
enter ev'ry trembling heart.

Breathe, O breathe thy loving Spirit
into ev'ry troubled breast;
Let us all in thee inherit,
let us find thy promised rest.
Take away our bent to sinning,
Alpha and Omega be;
End of faith, as its beginning,
set our hearts at liberty.
—Charles Wesley, "Love Divine, All Loves Excelling"

Once again, Lord, I see how your ways are best.
When we feel like we don't get the response

we need from someone, all we have to do is let love make up the difference. When life seems unfair and we don't think we are getting all we believe we deserve, we need to stop and let love make up the difference. As love makes a difference in our lives, so it can make a difference in our world. Keep encouraging us, Lord. Love will make a difference when it's your unending, all-encompassing kind of love.

Holy One, blessed is your name! Because nothing can separate me from your love, I have peace beyond all human understanding. The cares of this world are meaningless, because I can rest fully in the knowledge that you are watching over me, protecting me, and helping me. You are the light and the life, and your love is eternal. Praise be to God, for it is through your Son that I am saved. Amen.

There is nothing like the feeling of being loved, dear Lord, and I long to find someone to love me completely for who I am. I have a heart filled with so much love to give to others, so please send me a heart that is half full, and I will give of my own to fill it. I want to be of service, and I want to give back some of the amazing grace and love you have given me. Help me find those who would most benefit from my generosity and love, and guide me to them now. Thank you, Lord.

For God so loved the world that he gave his only Son, so that everyone who believes in him may not perish but may have eternal life.
—John 3:16

Love is the highest calling, God, and you have called me today to find love where there is only strife and confusion. You have asked me to rise to the challenge of loving those in my life who may not deserve it and to give love to those who may not believe it is real. Let me act in your honor, God, spreading the love I feel to anyone who needs it. Love is the gift that keeps on giving, and I have plenty of love to give. Amen.

Lord, only you can love unconditionally. Try as we might, we fall back into loving based on performance or loving based on being loved in return. Why do we make love a competition or an equation, Lord? Your love for us is unqualified, completely accessible, eternal. Dwell in our hearts and minds and direct our words and actions, Lord. Help us move ever closer to the unconditional way of loving that can change the world one heart at a time.

Who will separate us from the love of Christ? Will hardship, or distress, or persecution, or famine, or nakedness, or peril, or sword? As it is written, "For your sake we are being killed all day long; we are accounted as sheep to be slaughtered." No, in all these things we are more than conquerors through him who loved us. For I am convinced that neither death, nor life, nor angels, nor rulers, nor things present, nor things to come, nor powers, nor height, nor depth, nor anything else in all creation, will be able to separate us from the love of God in Christ Jesus our Lord.

—Romans 8:35–39